Unconscious
Basketball

UNCONSCIOUS BASKETBALL

Playing the Game for Keeps, Skills That Endure

BRUCE ROSENFELD, MD

Visit us at www.unconsciousbasketball.com

Cover and book design by Sean Ford

ISBN: 978-1-7337516-7-4

For my Dad, Philip Rosenfeld.
You were a really great coach.

TABLE OF CONTENTS

Contents

UNCONSCIOUS
BASKETBALL

Introduction:

NEVER FEAR FAILURE

Authors often begin books like this one hoping to impress the reader by claiming to have "once been just like you" then declaring for that reason "you'll relate to the upcoming pages." Maybe you are like me when I was your age, or maybe not, but I think you can benefit from this book either way. What I will tell you is that I started grade school without any problems or issues that I was aware of, but by the time I finished and was ready to move on to middle school, my constant smile and positive attitude was long gone. Maybe it was simply my age or possibly my surroundings, but in reality, I was bored and nothing was important to me or seemed to matter. I lacked a focus, something important in my life to put my energy into. I was sure that this lack of motivation had nothing to do with being afraid to fail, as it does for many young people. That wasn't my problem — my greatest fear has never been failing. What wakes me up at night remains a fear of mediocrity. Don't get me wrong — being less than great is fine if that's the endpoint on a path where you've given your full effort. No problem there. But if you've held back knowing you could have pushed harder and then performed without exception, to me that's far worse than failing.

This book is about learning lessons on the court that will help you for life, and this is your first lesson. Write it down and tape it to your mirror. Look at it every day. The concept is that important.

NEVER FEAR FAILURE
FEAR ACCEPTANCE OF MEDIOCRITY

You'll see many lessons like this throughout the book and often at the end of each chapter, so take note and do whatever you need to do to remember them.

Getting back to the start of middle school — in addition to the described boredom and confusion, I also now had a newly acquired athletic ability, most likely from the barrage of hormones that come at this age. Similarly, I possessed tons of energy searching for a direction, and like many young people, I risked the high probability of being steered down the wrong path. It didn't help that my new school exposed me to a whole range of distractions I hadn't seen before, including smoking, drinking, doing drugs, and stealing anything you could stick under your coat from the local stores. Even though I wasn't yet fully committed to this pathway — meaning I mostly just watched my friends carry out the deeds — I found that even being around this behavior was exciting. Finally, I was no longer bored, and that in itself was invigorating despite knowing the final outcome wasn't going to be something to be proud of. As the weeks and months passed, it became obvious that my role as bystander couldn't last forever, and I was getting closer to a commitment of my own. That's when through great fortune my life changed in that I found basketball, which jumped to the center of my world. Finally, in my mind, I had a purpose. Years later I wondered if it was possible that basketball had actually found me.

With the start of this new passion, I immediately loved everything that I did and everything about the game. I loved the coaching, the practice, the comradery, and the relationship between training and bringing these skills to a real-time performance. I wanted and pushed to become better and better and strove to become the best that I was capable of being. I knew full well that others may have had more innate ability, but I also knew that no one was going to out-prepare me. Basketball became my life, and I never looked back. Over the next five or six years, I ended up being a pretty decent high school player, and ultimately, I used the skills obtained on the court to go on to college and medical school before finally becoming a surgeon. A good number of my teammates and competition went on to play college ball, which I envied. However, at the time I knew that I couldn't follow that path because I understood I would never get into medical school with the associated time and energy commitment one needs to compete at that level. As much as not being on the court unsettled me, especially in the early years, I was thankful knowing the skills I learned had allowed me to succeed in so many other ways.

I wrote this book with the idea of teaching young players how to learn the game in a way so that the skills they gain and the inevitable success they find on the court ultimately has an impact on every challenge they'll face in life for years to come. Let's break this concept down, starting with basic offense.

- Jab, go left.
- Jab, go right.
- Jab, pull up, shoot.
- Jab, go left, spin back, pull up, shoot.
- Repeat again and again and again.

For hours, and usually at a solitary backboard, I practiced these moves over and over. I was convinced that the purpose of perfecting these skills was to teach me how to set up a play and score while being comfortable in any situation on the court. But I was way off. In reality, practicing these moves and playing the game itself were preparing me to get into medical school and become a surgeon. I learned to study and break down skills and motions, which I would then duplicate exactly. I learned about pride and working to be my best and giving my top effort, about loyalty and being a good teammate, and about being a part of something bigger than myself. I learned how to make those around me better, how to bring the team up to the next level, and how to understand what it means to suffer a setback then rebound stronger and in a better position than before. I learned how to put myself out there and how to be able to look at my teammate, win or lose, and say, "Hold your head up high; we did our best."

• • •

Without basketball, I have no idea where I would have ended up. Maybe basketball will bring direction to your life like it did for me. Maybe you want to be the best player in your area, like I did. Don't misunderstand, this book will teach you solid, practical instruction to become a very good, if not exceptional, basketball player. That will definitely happen if you take to heart these lessons. However, this book's true purpose is to point out the skills and habits that you will carry with you in other areas of life. For the moment, study and learn the game. It's that straightforward, and that's all you have to focus on today. We'll talk about that a lot. Understand that learning the game means you will need to practice. Practice correctly, practice disciplined, and then practice more and more. That's a theme you'll also see a lot as you go through these pages. By putting in the time, you'll reach amazing success on the court, but beyond that, learning the game will without question give you the skills for a successful career and a successful life. Pay attention, work hard, and focus. Commit yourself and recognize the first message.

NEVER FEAR FAILURE
FEAR ACCEPTANCE OF MEDIOCRITY

Chapter One:

WE ALL START SOMEWHERE

Arriving at the small waiting room, I couldn't help but notice there was no one else around. The day was Saturday, almost the end of the school year, but there was no secretary, no nurse, and no other patients. No one. My mom tried to make small talk with me when, finally, this lanky man with a sparse beard and ratty sweater walked out and said hello to us. After he shook my hand with a clammy grip, my mother said to us, "I'll be back in a while," obviously having worked out the details long in advance. The man squinted down at me while proceeding to make his formal introduction. But what exactly was going on? I had not been told anything, and in reality, wasn't sure where I was going that day when told to hop in the car. How did I end up in the office of a child psychologist? I had no clue.

It was the end of my final year at Moss Elementary School, and if I was being honest with myself, I hardly recognized the person that I was becoming. All of a sudden, I was fighting everybody. I fought other kids, my brothers, one or two at a time; it just didn't matter. It felt good to punch someone, and ironically, it felt good to get hit in return. I had worn glasses since the first grade, and to my parents' irritation, we were visiting the optician on a monthly basis to have the broken parts replaced. Maybe that's why I was being sent to the psychologist? Possibly to save money on fixing my glasses, but I doubted it. Things were definitely not going in the right direction.

I was in the fifth grade, and only a few weeks before, I had been suspended from school. Fortunately, it was for only one day. It didn't seem like such a big deal to me, but the principal viewed throwing rocks and trying to pick off kids on the playground differently. I had developed a pretty decent arm and was a pitcher on my little league team. When one of my friends knew that our teams would be up against each other within the upcoming week, he bragged nonstop how well he was going to hit against me. When the contest finally was in full swing, I faced my friend from the mound having decided long in advance that he would never get on base. So I hit him with the ball but not with the first pitch. For my first pitch, I threw the ball at my friend just to brush him back a little. He jumped out of the way in time to not get hit and gave me a dirty look. The second time, I connected with a fastball to his left hip. He had made it on base but not the way he had predicted. He wasn't happy. I laughed. Apparently, the principal wasn't happy with me hitting kids with rocks either, especially when one poor fourth grader had to go to the nurse's office with blood streaming down his shoulders. I wasn't sure how I was caught, but I was, and then I was suspended, which I thought was completely unjustified. Maybe going to the psychologist was the grounds negotiated for me to return to school. I was never told.

"Okay, Bruce, I'm Dr. Weinberg, and I've already had a long talk with your parents about what's been going on. I'm a child psychologist, and I see kids like you all the time. We're going to play some games and draw some pictures to try to figure out what's going on. Don't be afraid to tell me anything. I want to help you feel better."

I didn't respond. I was thinking, "I don't trust you and I don't like you, and this is the last place I want to be. What exactly does 'kids like you' mean? What kind of kid am I?" Not certain whether to cry or cover my head, I had this overwhelming urge to run from the building and hide.

"We'll start with you drawing a picture. Your folks told me you like to draw, so that works out well. I want you to draw a picture of a young boy, about your age. Just sketch someone you imagine and no one in particular. Tell me about his friends and what he likes to do. Let me know what frightens him and what he's worried about, and especially let me know if he likes his family."

Despite being eleven, it was apparent to me that the entire purpose of this drill was to push me into drawing and describing myself. I figured this guy wanted me to blurt out my darkest secrets and share my deepest thoughts. But how could he expect me to describe what was going on within me when I didn't understand it myself? As desperation morphed into annoyance and finally anger, my strategy changed as well. Should I go with my original plan and describe the perfect child, or should I define a troubled person angry at the world and with no clear path?

Confused and irritated, I chose to draw and describe the disruptive kid who hated everything and everybody. This took a while, and my inventions were accompanied by many discussions between Dr. Weinberg and me in which I talked and made up a lot of stories. It was entertaining at first, but eventually, I panicked, now worried Dr. Weinberg would conclude that the horrible person described in minute detail truly was me and that I was better off being sent away. By the end of this assignment, I could barely think and tried my best to hold back tears. Maybe there was something wrong with me after all.

Three hours and endless tests later, I was informed that it was okay to leave and that I wouldn't have to return. I was not prescribed any medication, and the psychologist never told me his conclusions or looked me in the eyes. I left his office feeling no different from when I had arrived, except that now I was happy to be outside in the comfort of the warm air. Summer vacation was only two weeks away, and I was about to move on from the security of Moss School, where I'd spent the last six years, to Franklin Middle School. Life was going to change drastically, and I wasn't even close to ready. I was hurting.

WE ALL START SOMEWHERE

• • •

Analyzing that incident years later, I realized that my life had approached a point where it could have gone in either a positive or negative direction. To say that I was at risk or considered highly vulnerable may have been an understatement. I was about to advance to the next phase where I would not be so sheltered, starting from an extremely poor position. Bored and direction-less best described me. None of this is uncommon for middle school or even high school kids, and you may be at this same place now. Or maybe not. Either way, keep in mind that if you are down as I was, or even lower, it's not without hope. You can pull yourself out — and don't be afraid to ask for help. Believe me when I say that no one has it completely figured out, even though from a distance it often might appear that they have.

WE ALL START SOMEWHERE

Chapter Two:

WE ALL HAVE CHOICES TO MAKE

First day, Franklin Middle School. No prior tours, no new student orientation, and no opportunity to meet our teachers before we showed up. As I walked through the front door, a feeling of sickness washed over me. No longer were we settled in with the same teacher for the whole day, in the same familiar classroom, surrounded by our same classmates sitting at our preassigned, comfortable desks. Franklin Middle School was different. There were new kids, different kids, many from the less sheltered parts of town. We changed classrooms and teachers for different subjects. During breaks and in between classes, we were expected to go outside on the playground, where unknowingly to any of us, the second part of our education was to take place. Talk on the playground was dominated by smoking and descriptions of partying. It didn't take long to learn that cigarettes, alcohol, and drugs were now a part of our world. No matter if we were prepared, we now all had choices to make.

"Can I have a smoke?" a kid would say.

"No, don't have any. I don't do that," I'd reply.

"You don't? Really? Yeah, I should probably quit" (words of wisdom from a thirteen-year-old).

Smoking? Partying? Why weren't we warned about this? All this was foreign and scary. Also, with the playground came fights — lots of them and pretty much every day. Girls and guys both whaled on each other, and these brawls were almost never broken up. There always had to be a clear winner and a clear loser, which undoubtedly would make or break your reputation. With fists flying and clothes tearing, kids instinctively formed a circle around the two combatants until an indisputable champion emerged or until blood began flowing a little too fast. Rarely were there repercussions. If you were strong and if you were tough and mean, you were held in high esteem. It helped your status even more to smoke cigarettes and drink alcohol. And you were at a different level altogether if you had any experience with drugs, whether that meant yourself or a family member. Kind of crazy but that's just how it was.

It had been a trying summer. The psychologist had reassured my parents that I was fine, but I didn't feel fine. And I certainly didn't want to go back to see him again. I was short-tempered and still highly conflicted. The neighborhood kids continued the daily pickup games of basketball, baseball, and football, depending on the mood and the ball available, but my interest was waning. I was becoming withdrawn without understanding why.

Starting middle school had been terrifying, and many of us felt pressure to fit in with a new group of kids. This crowd spoke differently, with rough language and a negative tone. I began to curse a lot, and soon I was wearing the designated sneakers and jean jacket that I had begged my parents to buy so I could blend in. It was obvious that I was being heavily influenced by peer pressure and was in trouble. There were a lot of choices to make, and more than anything, I wanted to be part of this group that seemed strong and confident, despite their obvious poor direction.

Weeks into the new school year, a routine was settling in, and I began to feel a little better. Unfortunately, that didn't last long. While hurrying outside to a class one day, I was shoved backward passing another kid who was surrounded by a lot of older friends. The hit wasn't damaging, yet this guy got up in my face and yelled for me to move out of his path. He then slammed me backward a second time as I staggered, trying to hold my balance.

"Hey, get outta my way!" he screamed, towering over me despite being only a little taller.

"Sorry." I hung my head.

"I think you meant it. You think you're tough?" He shoved harder, and again, I struggled not to fall — and not to cry.

This was new territory for me, being knocked around and outnumbered. Now inches away, this guy mouthed off again, saying he was going to seriously hurt me. I could almost taste his tobacco-saturated breath. I was deathly afraid. But suddenly, my panic turned to rage. My instincts took over, and with full force, I hit him directly in the jaw, knocking him to the ground.

Months of frustration and pain came flying out with severe intensity. With my heart pounding, I ran into the school, leaving my attacker surrounded by his gang, who stood in disbelief. My body was shaking. I was certain there'd be consequences, but I didn't know what to do, where to go, or what would happen next.

Later in class, I got word that I was expected to meet in an obscure lot after school to settle what I started. I agreed, but when the bell rang, I hauled myself home instead. I didn't tell my parents, and, as had become routine, I looked to my friends for answers. Finally, we came up with a plan: two of my closest buddies would act as my bodyguards at school. So for the next several weeks, I walked with these two large friends draped on either side. This seemed to work, and though we were often challenged, the three of us were not about to back down. The odds were always in our favor. Eventually, we blended in and were no longer bothered. Yet it was time to consider which path we were going to pursue regarding drugs and alcohol and other issues, and it didn't look promising.

Fortunately, basketball was about to rescue me from that life and provide the sense of purpose I'd been longing for.

We All Have Choices to Make

•   •   •

We all make decisions every day, and many have the potential to significantly affect our entire lives. It's not that a poor decision can't eventually be made right, but the problem is that the more wrong choices we make, the more difficult it becomes to straighten the path. People often say, "If I could only be eighteen years old again . . ." That would never be my wish since I can't be sure I'd end up in the same place I am now. I can't be certain things would have worked out again as they did. There are always decisions to make, and you should never be afraid to rely on people who have your best interest in mind to help you out.

It's not always easy to make the best choice, but think about what you are doing. Never be afraid to ask if you're not sure.

WE ALL HAVE CHOICES TO MAKE

Chapter Three:

DREAMS ARE IMPORTANT

At the start of gym class every afternoon we lined up, our eyes directed forward in eager anticipation of our orders. Years in the navy had shaped Coach Blindow's old-school style. As the boys' sole phys ed teacher at Franklin Middle School, Coach Blindow taught us about fitness and organized sports. But more importantly, he taught us his passion: basketball. From the first day we walked through the gym door, he shaped our thinking to mirror his mindset.

In addition to teaching physical education, Coach Blindow was the enormously successful coach for the Metuchen High School varsity basketball team. He worked with the players early in their development, teaching the middle school kids the fundamentals of the game with excitement and brilliance. Clinics were held Saturday mornings, and leagues went on throughout the year. The result was that after three years of intense instruction, the young players would move on to high school with finely honed skills. In fact, his coaching was so intense that his commands still echo in my brain:

> *"Dive for those loose balls."*
> *"Box out your man."*
> *"Dribble with your eyes up."*
> *"See the entire court."*
> *"Follow through on that shot."*
> *"Can't shoot, can't play!"*

From day one, it was apparent that basketball players were on top at the Franklin Middle

School playground. The stands surrounding the courts were generally filled with kids listening to music, talking trash, or just hanging out and watching the games. If you made a great shot before school or at lunch, word got around, and as you walked between classes, you got the proper respect. If you made a bad play, however, as I did once when my shot was blocked well into the crowded stands, you would hear about that mishap for what seemed like the entire year. Within the first month of middle school, I learned that I either had to smoke cigarettes, use drugs, become a much better fighter, or figure out how to shoot and handle the ball. As you probably know by now, I chose basketball, which fulfilled my needs and became my focus. With my newfound commitment, I made a promise to myself that I had every intention of keeping:

"I promise that within two years I will become the top point guard at Franklin Middle School."

That was my dream, and I was willing to commit fully to make it a reality.

DREAMS ARE IMPORTANT

● ● ●

To you, this promise may sound ridiculous or too simple, but I can assure you that it wasn't an easy objective considering where I was starting. What's more is that this promise represented the first time I had committed myself fully to any-thing. That was the true significance. I was ready to put in more hours and push harder than any other player, and I was confident it would hap-pen. With inspiration from Coach Blindow and the game itself, I finally had the desire to set a goal and work hard to achieve it. As the twelve-year-old me finally figured out, don't be afraid to set goals. The importance of this concept cannot be overstated. Don't be afraid to dream and think about where you want to be. And as always, don't be concerned about failure or working hard to reach that dream.

DREAMS ARE IMPORTANT

Chapter Four:

DREAMS ARE IMPORTANT; GOALS HAVE DEADLINES

I couldn't keep anything down. The mangled knots tortured my stomach, so much that I decided not to eat breakfast. This sick feeling would intensify in a few short hours when I'd find myself playing an impromptu pickup game that would set the tone for the rest of the week. I didn't know these guys, but they needed a sixth for a three-on-three game made up of players who claimed to be my age yet were far superior in both size and talent. I was terrified and didn't want to play, but you could never say no. Even more intimidating was that these kids played a street-style game, which I would need to learn quickly if I ever hoped to achieve any level of success. Pushed beyond my comfort zone, I wanted to turn around and go home. Thankfully, I didn't, because that action would have sent my life in an entirely different direction. While playing this game, I was barely able to hold my own. However, I was soundly awakened to where I needed to be.

The school year was finally over, and I was so excited thinking about going to All Pro Camp in a few weeks, run by NBA all-star Dave Bing and legendary college coach Howie Landa. Bing was at the top of his game, averaging over twenty-seven points for the Detroit Pistons, and Howie, nationally known for his incredible teaching skills, would go on to win the prestigious NJCAA Division I Basketball Championship for a second year in a row, which was almost unheard of.

After driving for what seemed like days, my exhausted parents struggled to get me settled into the tiny, rustic cabin furnished with eight double bunks holding thin, worn-out mattresses. Miraculously, we'd completed the three-hour drive to the Pocono Mountains despite the endless protests of my siblings. Our family wasn't good at taking long car rides, and my brothers entertained themselves by assuring me of my certain failure, relentlessly pointing out my inferior skills. Between the stomach pain and the continuous torment, I arrived with my confidence at undetectably low levels.

I ended up at basketball camp thanks to Coach Blindow's encouragement. All Pro Camp was the best. It had become a coveted destination, attracting top-tier Division I college players to an isolated venue for weeks at a time to play against one another and learn from the top coaches. These guys arrived from the University of Michigan, Syracuse, Vanderbilt, and Michigan State, just to name a few. Despite their status, the college stars were not only never pampered they also worked upward of fourteen hours a day, living in the same basic facilities as the campers. Most valued their experience, returning each summer to improve their game by competing against other top players and learning from the parade of coaches and NBA pros who would stream through as guests.

After formal introductions and shaking hands with my dad first, Bing looked in my direction and asked, "How old are you?"

Intimidated and not sure what to do with his outstretched hand, I looked toward the ground and mumbled, "I'm fine."

"That's good, but I asked how *old* you are."

I corrected my error, blurting out that I had just turned thirteen. I wasn't comfortable speaking with adults, especially those who could dominate other NBA players and stood over a foot taller than me. Overwhelmed with insecurity, I questioned how I'd survive the next two weeks. The other campers seemed to brandish a confidence I wasn't used to, and for good reason. Many

were from Detroit or Philadelphia or Washing-
ton, D.C., or other big cities and were accustomed
to playing ball on playgrounds in tough neighbor-
hoods. Despite my second home being the playground as well, it was different. These kids knew
exactly what was needed to get better, and they
competed with a hunger I'd rarely seen before. I
realized quickly that I needed to learn from them
to discover and harness that same passion within.

The next morning's wake-up call blasted at
7:00, though most of us had been far too excited
to sleep. We jumped off our beds, throwing on
ragged T-shirts that served as proof of time on
the court and proudly displayed our schools'
logos or favorite NBA teams. Shredded gym
shorts accompanied our torn-up tops though
rarely matched them, and if designated as lucky,
the same shorts may have been worn every day
despite the stench. My preference was solid,
white stretch socks pulled up to my knees, tightly
compressing my calves for comfort, and always
high-top sneakers — we all wore white Converse
(unless, of course, you were a Celtics fan and

wore black). Nothing about our dress was flashy, yet no one gave it a second thought. Attire was never equated to ability. Skill was best assessed by the look in a player's eyes and a confidence you could feel. Gear wasn't even on our radar.

Since it was a Monday morning, we were expected to spend twelve hours minimum on the court. The day started with instruction from a string of coaches, then practice, then more instruction and more practice, and finally league play somewhere around dinnertime. The games were physical and competitive with fouls rarely called. Being able to finish a shot while getting hit was expected. You learned to never look toward the ref for a break. At All Pro Camp, the focus was to get better, and so we hung on to every word, continuously asking the college stars and coaches as well as the NBA pros for their one-on-one assistance. They were happy to oblige.

Camp shirts were handed out upon arrival, and since these now were the nicest article of clothing most of us owned, we put them on right away. Although much appreciated, these shirts weren't the item we all wanted to go home with. A trophy was the real goal. These cheap plastic awards were hardly impressive; we understood there were only two ways to win one: you could be chosen as one of sixteen kids who made the all-star team, or your team could finish league play in first place. There were no trophies for second place and certainly no awards for participation. This is an important concept, and you should assess its value taking into account today's perspective. It was most important in our world and a code we lived by:

No Trophies for Second Place
No Awards for Participation

This statement summarized our culture at the time. We understood that only the top players would return to their hometowns with any sort of recognition. This meant that by week's end, when you got into your car empty-handed, you were forced to confront a reality. You could either accept the feeling of ineptitude — of not being good enough to take home an award — or you could commit to working harder the next summer. Most of us were ultracompetitive and chose the latter. We not only pushed ourselves to reach that goal, but we also pushed each other for the school year to come. Settling for "no trophy" was unacceptable, and even the possibility of finishing in second place was intolerable.

At the end of my first session at camp, I knew that Coach Blindow had sent me to the right place. All Pro Camp had given me the tools. It was now my job to put in the time and the focused effort to reach my goals.

DREAMS ARE IMPORTANT
GOALS HAVE DEADLINES

•   •   •

For all of us growing up, camp served to gauge our level of play and allowed us to compete against players from different backgrounds who possessed different skills with potentially higher expectations for their basketball careers. For you, travel team in addition to camp may serve this same purpose. Use this experience to ramp up your own intensity by tapping into the energy of the most competitive players you encounter. Don't be afraid to push yourself completely, knowing that you may fail in reaching the level you set your sights on. No one starts out perfectly, and you need to have the confidence that you'll reach your goal by out-preparing the others. Set your goals high and let yourself dream:

What if I become the top player in my school? In my town? In my state? What if I just want to make the junior varsity or varsity team — an enormous feat at my school?

The bottom line is that you'll become better from the experience — better on the court and better prepared for life. Don't be afraid to dream, as dreams are important. But now is the time to be methodical and to calculate exactly how you're going to reach that dream. That requires you to be focused, especially when the hard work comes in. Now marks the time to formulate a plan and push yourself.

DREAMS ARE IMPORTANT
GOALS HAVE DEADLINES

Chapter Five:

TAKE IT TO THE NEXT LEVEL

Franklin Middle School playground was home. This was our court, and to our good fortune, it was one of the few lit playgrounds in the area. The two full courts were almost always filled, and you could usually find any number of talented players until 10:00 each night when the lights shut off. On the rare occasion when we needed tougher competition, a road trip was initiated. Finding these games was word-of-mouth and therefore unpredictable.

At the start of our senior year, my friends and I had heard about an open gym in Linden, New Jersey, a tough town just outside of Newark known for its exceptional basketball teams. As the season was only a few weeks away, we thought testing our status would be a good idea. So, five of us made the trek. Unfortunately, we didn't carry much height compared to their players. Our tallest stood 6'3", but we were fast and had played together for years, confident in understanding one another's games. Under the direction of Coach Blindow, we were all sound players; each was a skilled shooter, and all could handle the ball. None of us shied away from a rebound. At this point, we had no concern about the match-ups, and we never thought twice about a pickup game — even in Linden.

Assessing the competition, we realized our best chance was to play the game in high gear. This came naturally, and so we won our first game with ease. The home crowd, of course, didn't appreciate outside players taking over their court time, but that didn't concern us. Winner stays on was the rule at this gym, as well as probably every court in New Jersey, and our team fully intended to play for several hours straight.

The second game began, and this team played more aggressively. The player covering me had a thick, muscular build and talked trash nonstop, which I figured was to compensate for his lack of skill. He wasn't a bad player; he just wasn't at the level he thought he was. His answer was to use his physical prowess to knock me around at every opportunity. I was far from being intimidated — he was nothing I hadn't been up against many times. But eventually, he started to get to me. Too much trash talk, too many dirty fouls, and too many times holding me. I decided that not only did I want to outplay this guy, but I wanted to embarrass him on his home court in front of his crowd.

As I pushed the ball up the court, I found myself on a one-on-one break against this self-proclaimed superstar. Unbelievably, his trash talk continued, even on defense, which fired me up even more. I shuffled the ball from my left hand to my right as I approached the basket then held it out. Take it away, I dare you. As expected, he lunged for my fake, allowing me to gently pass the ball behind my back and drift by for a soft lay in. I had practiced this move thousands of times, but I rarely used it in a competitive situation (and never in a formal varsity contest, as I wasn't fond of sitting the bench). The maneuver was effective. It not only resulted in a basket, but it also showed my opponent exactly what I thought of him.

"Walk!" he screamed. We both knew I hadn't.

"No way," I said, at which point he got up close and threatened to hurt me.

My guys had me covered and never would have let me get injured, but we were outnumbered and in a hostile gym. After a flurry of threats accompanied by pushing and name-calling, we decided to leave, happy to escape with our car intact and tires not punctured. On our way home, I reflected on how I'd played against my opponent. No, I hadn't traveled with the ball, but I knew very well that using that move would elicit that exact reaction considering where we were. Despite the guy deserving that treatment, I had completely disrespected my opponent, and he knew it. From my perspective, I had lost my composure and intentionally embarrassed my opponent to make him look bad. It was all about respect, and I showed that he deserved none. The message was received loud and clear, leaving him few options other than threatening me to try to keep his reputation intact. In that one play, I had shown that I was the better basketball player, thanks to years of working nonstop. However, I had lost my cool and embarrassed him, and as a result, we had to go home. Good players don't need to disrespect others, and that's where I went wrong. I wasn't proud of that action knowing that I had been taught differently. The best players are always in control.

TAKE IT TO THE NEXT LEVEL
WITH COMMITMENT AND PRACTICE

• • •

By senior year, I rarely walked into a gym or onto a playground anywhere in New Jersey without believing I was the best player on the court. I was certain that if I wanted to score or get to the basket, there was no one who could stop me — no matter how quick or how tall. In reality, I wasn't the top player on the floor in most cases, but that didn't matter. It only mattered how I perceived the situation since I always believed that got me ninety percent of the way to becoming the player I wanted to be.

How does one gain that level of confidence? How can a kid go from being an insecure, easily intimidated thirteen-year-old to a confident (bordering on arrogant) player unafraid to walk into any gym, even in the toughest parts of central Jersey? Again, the answer is simple:

- First, have a dream

- Next, make the commitment

- Third, have good teachers

- Fourth, be a good student

- And last, practice, practice, practice

We'll address this concept continuously in this book, so you can understand how it translates into much of life, too.

TAKE IT TO THE NEXT LEVEL
WITH COMMITMENT AND PRACTICE

Chapter Six:

TURN A NEGATIVE INTO A POSITIVE

"You just may not be college material!"

Frustrated, I listened as my sophomore English teacher accused me of cheating on a paper due that day. She said she felt sorry for me because I believed that I needed someone else to write the assignment for me. I hadn't cheated and actually worked hard to get a decent grade, but because I was a basketball player and hung around with other athletes — who were all considered less than academic — these accusations didn't surprise me. But it wasn't only the athletes who were stereotyped and discouraged from applying to college. Many of my classmates, especially the female students, were also pushed away, being told that college was not in their future simply because of who they were.

It's easy (and wrong) for anyone to make an assumption about an individual's future based on their appearance or family or friends, and it's the responsibility of each of us to push back and prove the accusers wrong. There will always be doubters, and when you're told that you can't, the response must always be, "Yes, I can. Just watch me."

A friend of mine, an accomplished orthopedic surgeon, relayed a story from the start of his premed studies. He grew up in a small town in Ohio, where he had worked from a young age at his family's modest clothing shop that specialized in neckties. Despite college being a financial burden for the family, they were happy to send him off since he'd always wanted to become a doctor.

Their excitement, however, was dashed after the initial meeting with his faculty adviser who told him that he was better off taking "some light business courses" and returning to the family store after graduation. After all, his adviser said, he was the first of his family to attend a university, and he "should be happy just getting a degree."

Four years later, my friend threw his Harvard Medical School acceptance letter on the desk of that same adviser, accomplishing his goal and proving the doubters wrong. He had been an athlete and had learned exactly what sports can teach:

- Dream first

- Then, set goals

- Finally, push yourself.

- And then, push yourself to the next level

The key to overcoming doubt and negativity, despite being told that your dreams are unrealistic, is to stay positive. Take a look at these examples you may hear when struggling to make a team:

> *"You're not fast enough." Okay, I'll do sprints.*
> *"You're not strong enough." Okay, I can lift weights.*
> *"You can't jump high enough." Plyometrics should work.*
> *"You're not tall enough." Okay, now I'm in trouble.*

The answer must always be the same - that you can. This is essential. Haters will be around forever, and the key is to use that destructive criticism to propel you forward. Note a sentiment attributed to Michael Jordan, yet many others have recited similar versions:

Turn a Negative into a Positive

I was bothered when my high school English teacher told me to forget about college, implying that I wasn't smart enough. In reality, it hurt because I believed she was right. She was hitting at my deepest insecurities, and it didn't feel good. As I began to consider my future at the start of my teenage years, I thought I'd probably end up in a college somewhere that wasn't challenging and only to play basketball — rarely to attend class. Up to that point, I had limited myself to easy classes, where just showing up earned you a decent grade. My thoughts about myself and my career goals, however, changed with one test.

On the first day of an SAT study course my junior year, we were handed a practice test. As expected, I did poorly. I was frustrated, and my response was a predictable "I'm out of here." My buddies weren't sure why I'd attended the class in the first place. Yet, eventually, I did take the SAT exam and despite not spending a single moment studying, I did well. Also, to my surprise, I did well enough to apply to the top academic colleges in the country. By this time, I was ready to leave my hometown and assert my independence.

During the fall of my senior year, my father and I traveled to Chicago to tour Northwestern University to see if the school was a good fit. I had no typing skills, so I had handwritten a single-page essay on my future goals and why I'd be successful. Printing neatly on the application page, I had talked about what basketball had taught me and the lessons that were now firmly embedded. I went on to describe how dedicating myself to the game had showed me how to set goals and attack them one at a time, no matter how big or how small. Surprisingly, the admissions team related to this heartfelt essay and decided to give me a chance. Having received my acceptance letter, I couldn't wait to make my way to campus after graduation. The reality was that I had no idea how horribly underprepared I'd be to compete in this high-pressure environment.

•

From the first day at Northwestern, I found myself competing against top students from all over the country. When I walked into finals the first quarter of my freshman year with two Bs and two Cs, I was nowhere near the perfect GPA needed to put me in the running for medical school. I did manage to pull up one grade and ended up with three Bs and one C. After a lot of self-reflection, I reassured myself that I had been down this road before, and if I applied the same principles I had before, I'd reach my goals.

- Have a dream

- Set a goal

- Stay committed

- Keep the focus

I knew this strategy had worked for basketball, and I was confident it would work for academics. That's how life went for the next three and a half years. I did well and I did keep my focus.

When it was time for applications to go out to medical school, I applied to several. But with a GPA on the lower end of those admitted (dragged down by a horrific freshman year) no school wanted to take a chance on me. I committed to apply again the next year, and this time I did get in. I wasn't about to let a first-year setback deter me; instead, I let it serve as motivation.

TURN A NEGATIVE INTO A POSITIVE

• • •

At some point before arriving at Northwestern, I realized that lessons learned from working on my game could easily translate to honing my academic skills, too. This is your takeaway lesson from this chapter.

Let's say you have an awful game — the most important game of the season and one against a rival team. How you handle this poor outing points to what type of person you are and what type of person you'll be for life. Do you give up and play even worse the next game, or do you get into the gym and work harder? The decision you make represents who you are and probably who you will be. But this mindset can be controlled by your actions. If you have a terrible game, your job is to pull yourself back from the situation and assess why things went so poorly. Ask your coach or your teammates for their assessment to learn where you can improve, and then get back on the court and work on your game. Never let a bad situation define who you are — instead, use it as a springboard to change and get better. This means you need to learn how to lose and how to address a negative. We'll go over that concept several more times in chapters to come. For now, know that you should never be afraid of failing; it can teach you a lot more than winning. Use it as motivation.

Turn a Negative into a Positive

Chapter Seven:

BECOMING PERFECT

It wasn't until college that I realized how much basketball had taught me about transforming a setback into a success, and how that could make me into a better student and ultimately allow me to get to medical school. Another important lesson I learned was exactly how much real-time commitment is necessary to achieve most worthwhile goals. Fortunately, this eye-opener was figured out early on, as you'll appreciate when you read further.

Most ballplayers in Metuchen learned early that you can never become too attached to your basketball shoes. After three to four weeks from purchasing a new pair, the ball of your pivot foot pushed into the rubber sole and your sock started poking through from the hours on the court. Unless you wanted to be severely injured, these shoes were done. The playground was brutal on your gear and certainly on your body. We also all had our own basketball, which was kept close at all times and generally lasted longer than our shoes, maybe six months. Despite the relatively short time together, you and that ball shared a deep connection. Somehow, we had convinced ourselves that the ball held power, and it was our job to unlock those tightly held secrets. We never doubted that it would take intense commitment.

Basketball is a game of timing and rhythm, and to maintain that skill, you have to attend to it daily. Ball-handling drills for a half hour each day and shooting for another hour — this didn't even include time playing one-on-one or five-on-five or whatever combination came up. Playing for hours was the obligation needed to "become perfect," and one we accepted without question. It felt strange not to play ball, and on that rare day you weren't on the court, your body just didn't feel right. But what does "become perfect" really mean?

Often, we're told that "practice makes perfect." You've probably heard this viewpoint in math or other classes to convince you to put in more time studying. This same statement is often corrected by sharp coaches, who counter that "practice doesn't make perfect, practice makes permanent," an interpretation from legendary football coach Vince Lombardi.

"PRACTICE DOES NOT MAKE PERFECT.
ONLY PERFECT PRACTICE MAKES PERFECT."

Then what does "become perfect" mean to a young player, and why is it important to work toward this goal? Or is it? John Wooden, head coach for the ten-time national champion UCLA, explained:

"PERFECTION IS WHAT YOU ARE STRIVING FOR, BUT PERFECTION IS AN IMPOSSIBILITY."

Admitting that becoming perfect is impossible, Coach Wooden then goes on to further qualify that statement and tell you what he really wants of his players by saying:

"STRIVING FOR PERFECTION IS NOT AN IMPOSSIBILITY."

Reading these assertions from arguably the greatest basketball coach of all time, one must then question why striving for perfection is important if reaching that target is impossible. Is it likely that simply pushing for this unattainable goal is all that is needed or should be expected from any coach? Is success simply measured by the effort put forth by the player, and that the "everyone gets a trophy" concept is actually the correct model for Coach Wooden? This is a difficult question and the answer is confusing. Let's go over this a bit more.

First, the "everyone gets a trophy" model, in its purest form, gives no credit to effort. The prize comes from simply being present and does not come from the commitment. In other words, if you show up, you get a trophy. It's that simple. Second, as Coach Wooden points out often in his descriptions of success, the trophy really has no value. An award is merely a by-product of success, and the trophy in itself is irrelevant. Certainly, as rookie basketball players at All Pro Camp, we were never sophisticated enough to understand that. To look at this differently, let's summarize by saying that success is not found at the end of the road and comes from the awards you may receive. Success comes from the changes and growth that occurs on the road itself. It wasn't the trophy for me at All Pro Camp, and it should never have been. For me, success was achieved long before the trophy was ever handed out that summer, coming from the hard work needed to reach that level. Coach Wooden summarizes this principle by saying:

"TRY YOUR HARDEST IN ALL WAYS AND YOU ARE A SUCCESS. PERIOD. DO LESS THAN THAT AND YOU HAVE FAILED. . . ."

As a person pushes to become a better player, that individual is being shaped wrestling the challenges that will undoubtedly be present. Working toward "being perfect" is the goal, yet it is also the reward. The honors received, if there are any, are unimportant. This is a hard concept for many of us to understand and even more difficult to accept.

During the final locker room scene in the popular football movie Friday Night Lights, Coach Gaines tells his team that he wants every player to get on the field and for the second half "be perfect." To his players' surprise, he states that even if they all are perfect for the remainder of the game, the team still may not win. How is that possible? How can the team play a perfect game and nonetheless lose? The answer lies in what was said next.

> "To me, being perfect is not about that scoreboard. . . . It's not about winning. It's about you and your relationship to yourself and your family and your friends. Being perfect is about being able to look your friends in the eye and know that you didn't let them down because you told them the truth — and that truth is that you did everything that you could."

BECOMING PERFECT: COMMITMENT, PRACTICE, FOCUS, DISCIPLINE

• • •

Adapting this attitude, there's no reason why we can't always strive to become perfect, every day and with every outing. This means that during practice and certainly in a game, you put in the complete effort to reach your goal. Commonly, you hear that players look forward to games rather than practice. For the great teams, it's almost entirely because practice is much more demanding than the games themselves. This is just what happens when you strive to be perfect; every session is a growth opportunity and should never be wasted. Whether you're an NBA star or the last player on your junior varsity team, you can learn and grow and strive to become perfect. Embrace this value system, and good things will happen.

Becoming Perfect:
Commitment, Practice, Focus, Discipline

Chapter Eight:

BECOMING PERFECT TAKES 10,000 HOURS

The "World-Famous Basketeers," brainchild of Coach Blindow and created for halftime entertainment, had just finished performing at the Duke vs. Maryland regular season matchup at Cole Field House. As the group ran into the stands, chased by a herd of overenthusiastic ten-year-olds begging for our autographs, we thought there could be nothing better. The performance had gone well for us — so well that programs were being thrust in our paths with the demand to sign as we moved back to our seats to take in the second half.

Our team had traveled several hundred miles, having been invited by Maryland as the entertainment for this televised rivalry. We were only a few years older than the kids who insisted on landing our scribbled names, but we were part of a team recognized as being special. And for good reason — we had put in the effort to reach this point.

Homeroom began at 8:30 a.m. at Franklin Middle School, and most days the Basketeers were at practice by 7:15 a.m. This went on until the bell sounded, when we ran off to class to avoid a late mark. A lot of time was spent perfecting ball handling, which the fans appreciated most. We practiced making the effort smooth and without change in the cadence: twirling the ball around the back and quickly moving to the left then to the right; and shifting the ball through the legs forward then backward, to the left, and then to the right — all at game speed.

The Basketeers commanded the attention of all those in the arena wanting to see young kids press their skills and well-choreographed performances beyond the norm. Our opening routine started with music blaring, followed by twenty kids running full speed on the court in four groups, one by one skating in for behind-the-back layups. Our ages ranged between eleven and thirteen, and our dedication couldn't be mistaken. Fans delayed their trips to the concession stands, turning their heads to see exactly what this group was all about. When we started spinning the basketballs on our fingers — twenty all at once — that's when the show really began.

Every day we were scolded, "Don't play with the basketball in the house!" But I did. We all did. We couldn't help ourselves. It took that kind of 24-7 attachment to the ball to perform comfortably in front of 15,000 fans. How else could you get twenty middle school kids to effortlessly spin a basketball and perform other tricks for a good amount of time and in front of so many people?

After we mastered spinning the ball on our fingers, we wondered why we had only used an index finger for this trick. How about a thumb, or a knuckle, or a rock, or a coin? How about a ballpoint pen? And from there - how about taking that same pen and holding it with your teeth, pulling your head straight back? We racked our brains to discover the most creative possibilities. On one rainy day when practicing ball handling in my basement, a broom caught my eye. I promptly sawed off the head and then drilled a hole in the top of the broom handle for the pen to rest in tightly. Now I had a spinning ball atop a six-inch pen popped into the hole of a four-foot wooden broom handle that was held two feet straight above my head. By the next week, Coach Blindow fit this into our routine. The four captains had all sawed off brooms and painted the sticks red, white, and blue. It became a highlight of the performance.

Despite the Basketeers being created for show, the ball-handling skills we perfected improved our real games tremendously. What the routines represented was significant. The learning and synchronization of these tricky sequences demonstrated deep commitment. You simply couldn't reach that level without putting in the hours. If by age eleven, you could run the length of the court dribbling at full speed and flip the ball behind your back in either direction without missing a step, you were at a different level. Both individually and as a group, the Basketeers were impressive. The captains were skilled players and were learning to be leaders. Yet, no one was more exciting and demonstrated more promise than a kid who had recently moved from Perth Amboy, New Jersey — Bradley "Showboat" Sellers.

Perth Amboy intimidated. Rough town not too far from us; tough kids, great athletes, all business.

It was no surprise that Bradley was quickly recognized for his superior talent. Fortunately for us, he had moved to Metuchen at the start of middle school, and we wouldn't have to play against him at any time in the future.

Pressured to keep up with older brothers, Bradley was faster and stronger than anyone close to his age. Whatever he attempted on the court appeared effortless and natural, whether with the Basketeers, or as a varsity athlete, or on the playground, where Brad was a legend and dominated. The pressing question is — how did Bradley reach this level? How did he become dominant? Was it simply natural talent, or was this earned by putting in the time? Or was it both? And if this skill was all earned, what was the commitment needed? After all, you can't teach someone to be 6'3" and have lightning speed. (Or can you?)

My take is that Bradley did have natural ability and a lot of it. But I believe it was the time spent perfecting his craft that made him so successful.

That's what allowed Brad to "become perfect" and be an amazing ballplayer.

There is a widely accepted theory that it takes 10,000 hours of practice in most anything to reach an exceptional skill level. We'll go into this a bit more later, but taken at face value, Bradley reached his 10,000-hour mark early in his career. Most of us hit that goal a few short years after. This commitment can be best analyzed from a recent conversation with Bradley and corroborated with a few of my buddies.

> "Back in the day, how many hours did we spend at the playground? Let's say on days that we didn't have school."

To a man, the response was that we'd arrive early in the morning and most of the time didn't leave until late that night. Breaks were taken on and off, especially when we'd walk over to a nearby convenience store and each buy a half-gallon container of lemonade to stay hydrated. During the week, we'd often get there around four in the afternoon and stay until lights out at ten – usually breaking for a few hours for dinner. Brad then spoke about what he did on those rare days at the playground when no one else was around.

"Bruce, I just did drills over and over. Things Coach Blindow taught us. Dribbling, shooting, working on your strength, and getting over the rim. Then when people did show up, I'd play one-on-one, two-on-two, five-on-five. Played against anyone. Younger, older, it didn't matter. Just played with whoever showed up. Loved it when the older players got there or the kids from Perth Amboy or New Brunswick or any other town."

I added that I remember playing him one-on-one full court, games to eleven. In this situation, you certainly had to get back on defense. I then asked Brad if he ever got bored.

"Never. You've got to love the game. You have to love being on the court and love being at the playground. It just has to not feel right if you don't have a ball in your hands."

BECOMING PERFECT
TAKES 10,000 HOURS

• • •

In his best-selling book Outliers, Malcolm Gladwell devotes a full chapter to the "10,000 Hour Rule." He attributes much of an individual's or group's success — including the Beatles, Bill Gates, and professional athletes — to skills and opportunity, but even more so to the time put in to sharpen that endeavor. In other words, time spent perfecting the craft. According to Gladwell, the essential number seems to be 10,000 hours and I think that our experience supports that theory.

That was Bradley's experience and mine as well with my own game. The same rule applied when I trained to become a surgeon. Let's take a look and see how this played out, specifically adding up the numbers, starting with basketball.

By age eleven, most of us practiced three to four hours each day during the week, including games and drills. We usually spent one or two of those hours shooting or dribbling on our own (including our jab series), and the rest of the time was spent in game-time situations. We easily doubled this commitment on weekends and tripled it during the weeks of summer vacation. For me, I calculated that I had reached my 10,000 hours by age seventeen, but I know that Bradley reached his 10,000 hours years earlier.

You're probably wondering where you possibly can come up with that amount of time to practice. Today, schedules are so overbooked, and school expectations are much more demanding. Yet, there may be time if you focus and cut back on activities that aren't as beneficial. You won't like hearing this, but many studies point out that teenagers spend up to nine hours per day on social media, while those slightly younger spend up to six. Pulling away from these norms will not be easy, but if you can, you'd have plenty of time for other efforts, like mastering your basketball skills. It's your choice to make, but if you want to develop a skill way beyond the level of your peers, you will need to find those 10,000 hours somewhere. It takes practice in "becoming perfect," and as we know, it's not just any type of practice but perfect practice. Without trying to sound judgmental, my recommendation is to find the time to reach that level if it's that important to you. If you become one of the few who possess that type of self-discipline, your success on the court is almost guaranteed.

BECOMING PERFECT
TAKES 10,000 HOURS

Chapter Nine:

CONFIDENCE MUST BE EARNED

"Thanks for coming to see me today," the surgeon says at your follow-up appointment.

"The CT scan shows a growth in your kidney, and the problem is that it's probably cancer. The good news is that if we can fully remove the mass, you'll likely be cured and nothing else will be needed."

"Oh, okay," you reply, "I guess not great news but not as bad as it could be. You're a surgeon, you can get this out of me, right?"

The doctor looks down. "Yeah," he replies, speaking softly. "I think so. Well, maybe. Usually this works out, but it may not. I don't know. If you want, I guess we can give it a try."

Not very reassuring, is it? With that answer, you (and most patients) would run from the office and not allow this doctor anywhere near you with a scalpel. And no one could blame you. Why not? Because it is painfully obvious that this surgeon lacks confidence. He demonstrates a complete uncertainty of his skills. Confidence is essential in being a competent surgeon. In fact, it may be one of the most important traits. It is also fundamental to becoming a good ballplayer.

Even as a kid, I understood how important confidence was to my game. Growing up, the walls of my bedroom were filled with handmade signs I had written on construction paper to be sure I absorbed the sentiments. None was more important than this statement that hung directly over my bed:

SUCCESS ON THE COURT IS
90 PERCENT IN YOUR HEAD

Why was this important? What exactly did this mean? It meant that if you look at your opponent for even a second and think they're better than you, your chance of coming out on top in the contest is minimal. To be successful, you need to feel confident, understand your strengths as a player, and try to figure out the vulnerabilities of your competition. As I've already described, at every court I walked onto in New Jersey, I was convinced that I was the best player on the floor. This was far from the truth, but I knew that this type of confidence was needed to compete at the level I desired. Of course, having confidence is important and fundamental, but it's also important that the confidence is earned. Otherwise, it's just empty arrogance.

YOU MUST HAVE CONFIDENCE
YOU MUST KNOW THIS CONFIDENCE IS
EARNED

The feeling of deep self-assurance has to be a part of your fiber and woven into each and every cell. Most important, this confidence must be deserved; you should never feel entitled. How does one reach this point in becoming a skilled basketball player, and for that matter, a surgeon as is my profession today? There's only one way, and it's the same for sports, medicine, and really anything else in life: through preparation and commitment. Let's analyze this concept of earned confidence by now looking at the path necessary to become a surgeon.

Accepted to college for premed studies, I statistically had a very low chance of being admitted to medical school four years later, calculated at one in seventeen. Four years at Northwestern and eventually medical school admission was achieved. The first two years of medical school were spent in the classroom with instruction at a pace five times faster than college. There was a fair amount of pressure, but again, my commitment remained strong. The last two years of medical school were spent on rotations as "junior doctors." Your responsibility depended on the rotation (surgery, pediatrics, psychiatry, etc.), and you worked close to eighty hours per week. Testing at the end of each rotation was not only a written exam but also an oral one. This meant you sat with an attending physician (the specialist who trained and supervised you during your rotation) for usually thirty minutes to an hour, with any topic being fair game. There was lots of pressure, and you couldn't cut corners. That examiner probably figured out whether they were going to pass you for that rotation within the first two minutes of the session.

Then came acceptance into residency. This is where you learn how to really practice medicine and perform surgery. Every other night on call for the first two years meant you'd arrive at the hospital at 5:00 a.m. on most days and usually leave to sleep at home thirty-nine hours later. An average workweek was 140 hours, and during this time in the hospital, you made hundreds of decisions, most mundane but many life-and-death. You also performed many high-risk surgical and invasive procedures and were 100 percent responsible for all your actions and decisions. A poor outcome, missed diagnosis, or less than optimal procedure not only was grounds for dismissal but may also have resulted in a malpractice lawsuit. Yes, there was pressure, but again, you pushed on. Surgery training had taught you how to care for the deathly ill and handle trauma of all kinds, including gunshot wounds and stabbings, as well as perform elective surgeries while sleep deprived. After two years of general surgery came three years of specialty training — urology, in my case — and now you were on call every night. You understood that in a few years, you would be in charge, and people and staff would be looking to you for support, answers, and leadership. It was your responsibility to learn all you could to become a well-trained, capable surgeon before graduation. That was on you.

INTENSE COMMITMENT IS HOW YOU EARN CONFIDENCE

By the second year of surgical training, the hours we'd clocked had reached well over 10,000. We had put in the time, made the commitment, and as a result, earned the exceptional confidence to become skilled surgeons. With 30,000 hours of training under our belts at graduation, we had blown up the "10,000 Hour Rule." It was a nice feeling, and the confidence we earned was necessary. In many situations, it often was a matter of life and death, as in this next case in point as a senior resident.

During my fourth year post medical school training and well into my residency training, a fifty-eight-year-old man came to the urology clinic after noticing several episodes of thick blood in his urine. The urology fellow, who was still in training but very high in rank, assessed this person and ordered all the appropriate studies. He discovered a large mass in the man's kidney, which looked like a cancerous growth. The fellow had recommended removing the kidney, and the procedure was scheduled. As it was the start of the fellow's new position, he was excited for the opportunity to perform this complex operation.

As a senior resident, I was to be the second assist in the case, which meant that I did little more than hold retractors so everyone else could see. The junior resident, a good friend of mine, would be way down at the end of the table and barely able to do anything important but was still expected to be present. The case was set up right away, went smoothly, and was completed in record time. The fellow was pleased with himself, having just removed his first kidney at this new location, with minimal blood loss and demonstrating excellent surgical skills. The attending physician left us to close the incision with the fellow, thanked everyone, and was out the door long before the patient was to be transferred to the recovery room.

As residents, we were expected to write the post-op orders and care for the patient until he was discharged. Happy to be finished so quickly, we hoped that we'd even get home at a reasonable hour that day and congratulated the fellow on his success. Everything in the room was great, and we were plugging along routinely when the tone drastically changed. The monitors started screeching loudly in panic, signaling that our patient's blood pressure had plummeted to dangerously low levels. Thinking there was some malfunction with the equipment, the anesthesiologist checked the patient's vital signs with a manual technique and confirmed the monitor readings. It became obvious that our patient was fading, and we didn't know why.

The OR nurses frantically tried calling our attending, but he was long gone and couldn't be reached. With the patient's blood pressure critical, the fellow feverishly reviewed the possibilities. With no one of higher rank in the room, it was up to the fellow to decide on the next move. His thinking was that the patient was experiencing a massive heart attack or some other issue with his heart or lungs — a reasonable conclusion, but the junior resident and I didn't agree. We suspected a bleed and argued with him to explore the man's abdomen immediately. The fellow opposed our assessment and forbade us to open the wound. Instead, he ordered the patient transferred to the recovery area for further evaluation and care. When we again challenged the fellow on his decision, he repeated this statement and left the operating room abruptly. The anesthesiologist, junior resident, and I began to carry out his orders, yet the patient's blood pressure was barely registering. We knew that our patient was about to die, and we were losing the ability to resuscitate him.

With the situation now even more critical (if that was even possible), I made the decision that now I was the ranking surgeon in the room (even though it had been only a few short minutes since the fellow left). After a brief exchange with my junior resident, we agreed to open the patient against the direct orders of our superior. We both felt convinced enough at this point that we were ready to take the heat if we were wrong — a mindset learned from my years of general surgery training and before then on the court.

Make a Decision It May Not Be the Right Decision, But Make Your Decision and Stand by It

Quickly, we washed the abdomen with iodine and began the procedure. The patient's wound burst open as we sprung the staples and cut the thick fascia. Liters of blood overflowed, making it difficult to know where the bleed was coming from, so we threw pads into the wound that absorbed the fluid almost immediately. Assuming the bleeding could only be coming from the main renal artery, I was able to blindly explore the area and find the source, actually feeling the blood pulsating unhampered. From there, we tied off the bleeding vessels and the patient responded.

CONFIDENCE MUST BE EARNED

• • •

Opening the patient and exploring his abdomen proved to be the right decision, and waiting even a few more minutes probably would have resulted in this man's death. As the junior resident and I were closing the abdomen, the fellow came back into the operating room to find out why we hadn't made it to recovery yet, and we filled him in on what had happened. Ultimately, the patient did well and was able to go home in three days. He was back to full activity within the month.

Going against the direct word of a superior would have had serious consequences if we were wrong. I might have even been thrown out of the program for my actions. But it was the right thing to do, and looking back (though not appreciating this at the time), I know that making that decision took extreme confidence. But how could I possibly have had this level of self-reliance at such an early stage of my training? The answer is simple: it could only have been the time commitment devoted to the skill. With over 20,000 hours of training logged in, the confidence I'd gained was earned and well deserved.

This is what you need to take from this story: that there are no shortcuts to gaining confidence. You have to work on your game to the point where you know that you're at a completely different level because of your commitment. Don't ever feel entitled and never expect handouts. True confidence comes with a deep price, but when attained, no one can take that away. I earned my confidence by spending the hours in the OR, and in reality, it allowed me to save this man's life. If it was simply unearned arrogance, meaning if I had not put in the time to know what was needed, the outcome would have been much different. That I am sure of.

Work hard and realize that the most important person you need to convince of your true capabilities is yourself. Did you work to "become perfect"? Can you look at your friends and your coaches and teammates and say without reservation that you did all you could to become successful? Most importantly, can you look yourself in the mirror and say yes to that same question? Nothing comes for free, but nothing feels better than hard work and the confidence gained from it.

CONFIDENCE MUST BE EARNED

Chapter Ten:

TEAM FIRST ALWAYS

I've got 20 percent of my crew who are completely behind me for whatever I do. This is the core I can always count on, and they'll push forward with or without me. Great bunch. The next 60 percent will do what it takes but usually require a little work. They're just fine. It's the last 20 percent who drive me crazy. This is the group that no matter where we're going, somehow, they just can't get there easily. They take up most of my time and siphon most of my effort. The reality is, if we can pull this last bunch along, if we can get them on board, especially early on, things really happen.

The quote you just read (I'll reveal the source in a bit) shows the importance of putting the team before anything else. The concept of "team first" is simple. It's understanding that the needs of the group are more important than those of an individual player. Great teams always figure out how to work together. Recently, I spoke with Coach Pat Fitzgerald, the highly successful head football coach at my alma mater, Northwestern University. If you're not familiar with Northwestern, despite having only 9,000 undergraduate students, it's a part of the Big Ten Conference in which most schools are state funded and have a much larger enrollment. In addition, Northwestern is consistently ranked prominently alongside the Ivy League schools and other top-tier universities in academics, which also limits the number of athletes the school recruits. Yet despite its small size and rigorous academics, Northwestern competes week after week against powerhouse athletic programs such as Ohio State, University of Michigan, Wisconsin, and Penn State.

In my conversation with Coach Fitzgerald, he told me that there will always be players ready to work hard from the first day of practice, starting their freshman year. And then there are others who need more input but still will be fine. Finally, there's the group who's most difficult to figure out and hard to reach. They're tough and need a lot of attention. This sounded really familiar to me and you'll soon see why.

The opening paragraph from this chapter could easily have come from my discussion with Coach Fitzgerald, but it didn't. This account came from the CEO of a successful medical group in the Midwest made of thirty-five physicians, many physician assistants, and over 250 employees. Looking at a college football program, it's easy to understand how young, newly liberated freshmen may not jump right into the team concept with the start of the season. But the situation described by this healthcare CEO involved experienced, accomplished professionals who, despite being well educated, couldn't seem to work for the betterment of the group. These doctors understood the importance of the commitment intellectually, but somehow, they just couldn't make it happen. Unfortunately, this situation is typical for most groups.

The reality is that most basketball teams will never reach their full potential. That would take thoughtfulness, sacrifice, and above all, discipline. It would also involve pushing ego aside, the hardest task for skilled professionals in any field.

TEAM FIRST ALWAYS REQUIRES A FOCUS ON SELFLESS ACTIONS

This concept needs to be ingrained early because it can be difficult to acquire later in life. As a point guard, that was my job — focusing on team first. This next story demonstrates that exact concept one time during my senior year when I was asked to play a different role for one game:

It was just a few hours before a tough out-of-conference matchup, and we were set to play a streetwise team from Newark, New Jersey. Fortunately, the game was at home, but I was still concerned, especially because we were down our two top scorers, who had the flu. Coach approached me before the game and asked me to make up the difference in scoring, and despite being the point guard, to put up big numbers.

"Bruce, I need you to get some points tonight. We don't have much firepower with your buddies out."

"You don't have to ask me twice to shoot the ball more," I said. "This is going to be fun!"

That night, I scored thirty-six points, and the Metuchen Bulldogs won pulling away. I was well aware that I could have scored much more than the eleven points I averaged, but most games I didn't shoot much, fully understanding as a point guard that wasn't my primary purpose. My job was to get the team involved and to elevate the other players' games. Points got your name and often your picture in the local paper. Points helped your stats and fed your ego, but scoring points wasn't my job. It wasn't my role, and it wasn't best for the team.

TEAM FIRST ALWAYS: THOUGHTFULNESS, SACRIFICE, AND DISCIPLINE

It's obvious how self-centered play affects a basketball team, but how can it influence other teams, especially teams that have nothing to do with sports? Let's look how it affects my colleagues and me in medicine. This is a very important area that we could improve upon.

Most doctors don't buy into the "team first" ideal. Worse than that, there often is a small cluster of doctors in any physician group who consciously or unconsciously works against it. This same small band tend to be the most vocal and often the most influential. Yet, for the betterment of the group, the goal is to bring these doubters into the fold early and teach them to be team players. Unfortunately, this also goes against traditional medical training.

From the start of medical school, physicians are taught that it's their job to be superheroes. This means that when a problem comes up, it's the doctor's sole responsibility to swoop in and save the day, and do it alone. For example, if there's an issue in the operating room and you're the surgeon of record, it's your responsibility to fix it. We're not taught that it's a "team problem," or we all need to "figure it out together." That thinking is just never present. Physicians are expected to be the player that averages forty-five points per game. That person may take thirty shots and no one else even touches the ball. But that doesn't matter since it's that physician's job to bring home the win, single-handedly if needed. Only in recent years has this thinking begun to change in real-izing that the team approach may be more effec-tive. In medicine, old habits like the "superhero" mindset need to be unlearned.

TEAM FIRST ALWAYS: THOUGHTFULNESS, SACRIFICE, AND DISCIPLINE

Let's now look at another real-world example in which the focus and need to be a team player is unparalleled: an EOD technician. EOD stands for explosive ordnance disposal. These extraor-dinary military members literally work to make the world safer for all of us, as it's their job to respond to threats to our country from any source. This means conventional explosive, bio-logic, or nuclear. These professionals work closely with various special operations forces and war-fare units as well as Secret Service. Because EOD technicians need to go anywhere there's a threat, they must be able to jump out of planes carrying heavy equipment and dive deep into the ocean – essentially go wherever they are needed. Success is paramount, and this can't happen without a team, and a team can't work without complete trust.

So, how is the team concept taught when adapting these rules is critical to survival? And can this culture be translated to the civilian world — or even the world of basketball? Let's look at the viewpoints recently detailed to me by an extremely knowledgeable and conscientious EOD technician. The concepts are divided into four categories for clarity. Think about them carefully and think how these can relate to your own team, in your own world.

THE CONCEPT OF TEAM

• Each member must mindfully accept that the team is stronger than the individuals on their own

• The sanctity of the team is deeply ingrained and it's expected you'd sacrifice yourself (including your life) for the team

• All members must understand the team's goals and mission and be completely accepting of it

THE ROLE OF TEAM LEADERS

• Leaders must be role models and strive to set a good example at all times

• Leaders are never "off the clock"

- What's done on a Saturday night impacts performance during work hours

LEARNING AND CHANGING TEAM CULTURE

- The team culture is taught in a subtle manner, meaning from top to bottom

- Culture is taught by example not instruction

- Improvements start at the bottom (from those performing the tasks) and work up to the top

- It is acceptable to critique your colleague

- All criticism must be constructive

- It is not acceptable to demean or discourage any team member

TEAM STANDARDS AND EXPECTATIONS

- The team must set standards and expectations, and everyone must completely understand them

- Each team member must understand the consequences of not meeting the accepted standards

- The group must be able to remove the members who can't meet the standards and are, therefore, not suited for the job

- The group needs to be able to remove anyone who does not accept the goals or embrace the team concept

Think carefully about what these concepts mean for you and your team. If you can apply these ideals with the same urgency as those in the military, you're guaranteed success. Even though much will depend on the coaching staff, players like you can bring about these values in a subtle way, with a tremendous response.

• • •

We define ourselves by our actions, and we must all decide if we want to be a team player or the person who focuses only on their own stats. For example, we've witnessed the player who reflects on how and why the team lost after a game, yet we've also seen the player who consistently runs to the scorer's table to check on their point totals whether the team has won or lost the game. Most of us understand the concept of team, but few live by the standard. Why is that? Because being self-centered is easier, and it takes less thought and less discipline. A group full of selfish individuals may find some success, but it's guaranteed that they won't reach their full potential. For most, mediocrity and less than full effort is acceptable. We all must decide where we want to fit in, but truly great teams know that success happens only when working together.

TEAM FIRST ALWAYS: THOUGHTFULNESS, SACRIFICE, AND DISCIPLINE

Chapter Eleven:

YOU'LL NEVER LEARN HOW TO WIN UNTIL YOU LEARN HOW TO LOSE

No one likes to lose. Somehow, we find this degrading and view ourselves and our team as a failure if we don't have a winning record. We all want to be seen as dominant and labeled as winners because it makes us feel good about ourselves. But is winning always best for growth? Exactly how do we get better as individuals? How do we grow as a team? The easy answer is that progress happens faster when we face adversity, when we hit an obstruction and then overcome the challenge. Friedrich Nietzsche, the often quoted nineteenth-century German philosopher, is attributed as saying:

"WHAT DOES NOT DESTROY ME, MAKES ME STRONGER."

Think about what that means for yourself, either on the court or in daily life. It describes that when you suffer a setback, or when you get knocked down, your job is to get back up and be stronger. This will help you become more prepared for the next challenge that is certain to come your way.

Pat Conroy, in his autobiographical novel *My Losing Season*, gives the following testimony on why losing a basketball game can teach you so much more than winning it. See if you agree.

"Winning makes you think you'll always get the girl; land the job; deposit the million-dollar check; win the promotion, and you grow accustomed to a life of answered prayers. . . . Loss is a fiercer, more uncompromising teacher, cold-hearted but clear-eyed in its understanding that life is more dilemma than game, more trial than free pass. . . . I learned much, much more from loss."

Loss not only taught Pat Conroy how to be a better ballplayer, it also taught him how to cope with the inevitable afflictions or failures that will undoubtedly occur in one's lifetime. There has not been another player who has understood the power of using a defeat as a propellant better than Michael Jordan. As detailed in an article by Kevin Sherrington in the Dallas Morning News, 1998, the legend has been retold that the young man, then called Mike Jordan, was cut from his varsity team for another player named Leroy Smith. The important takeaway lesson is not whether Jordan was left off the team, but what Jordan did when convinced he was slighted.

As a sophomore, Mike Jordan was among fifty kids trying out for basketball at Laney High School in Wilmington, North Carolina. Laney had a solid program in which, traditionally, the top fifteen kids made varsity, and the next fifteen would play on the jayvee squad. Tenth graders were rarely placed on varsity as a rule, and this year, one spot did remain open for a sophomore. "Pop" Herring, a successful young coach, chose 6'7" Leroy Smith over 5'10" Mike Jordan, not for his superior talent, but for his height, leaving Jordan on the jayvee squad to seethe about this choice. By all accounts, this decision was successful, in that the next year, Jordan was a star for the varsity, tallying consistent forty-point performances, and by his senior year, he was offered a scholarship from Coach Dean Smith to play for the University of North Carolina.

Turning a negative into a positive has been Michael's way. He learned to use the adverse situation as a focus to push him forward — a skill he perfected early. In his Basketball Hall of Fame enshrinement speech, Michael Jordan thanked a multitude of players and coaches for putting a real or perceived obstacle in his path, and as a result, "placing another log on the fire," implying that he would never have achieved his great success without these insults. In his acceptance speech, he first acknowledged Leroy Smith for making the varsity squad instead of him, but then he thanked many others:

- Buzz Peterson, for being chosen as North Carolina's high school player of the year over him their senior year

- Coach Dean Smith, who wouldn't let him appear on the cover of Sports Illustrated with his teammates, not because he was undeserving, but solely because he was a freshman

- Bulls owner Jerry Reinsdorf, who wouldn't let him come back soon enough from a broken ankle to "protect his long-term investment"

• Coach Doug Collins, who tried to stop him from playing basketball in the summer due to his interpretation of "team rules"

• Coach Pat Riley, who wouldn't let him hang out with his closest friends and New York Knicks players Patrick Ewing and Charles Oakley because he was supposed to be their "enemy on the court"

• Coach Jeff van Gundy, who maligned him by saying that he "conned and befriended" the players before games in order to attack them on the court

• Bulls general manager Jerry Krause, for impressing on him that "organizations and not players win championships"

• Bulls assistant coach Tex Winter, for pointing out that there's no i in team (to which Michael countered that there is an i in win)

- Bryon Russell of the Utah Jazz, who had the nerve to claim while Michael was in the midst of playing AA baseball that he'd "shut him down" if he ever came back

Michael then went on to explain how he used these setbacks to maintain his focus.

> "As a basketball player, I'm trying to become the best that I can. And for someone like me, who has achieved a lot over the time of my career, you look for any kind of messages that people may say or do to get you motivated to play the game of basketball at the highest level."

Listening closely, you hear that Michael had such a high level of success by turning the negative into a positive. Of note was that he often had trouble finding the negative for motivation on a day-to-day basis - motivation that he could use to "place another log on the fire." But Michael always found something, and for the less than superhuman player, these negative events are always present. It is up to the individual to use them to improve — to get to the next level.

You Can't Learn How to Win until You Learn How to Lose

• • •

For your own basketball goals, it is essential that you learn exactly what you did wrong before you take on that same challenge again so you don't repeat those mistakes. Meaning, after a loss, listen to your coaches, study the videos if available, and physically write down how you can improve as an individual and as a team. Did you have too many turnovers? Was your shot selection poor? Did you forget to cover for one another on defense, or play as a team? Then work to change those problems. Again, this is not just basketball we're talking about, but it's about developing habits for life as well. Fortunately, you only are being asked to improve your basketball skills right now, but I promise you, the reward will ultimately be much greater.

To summarize, never be afraid to lose, for in the long run, it may be the best thing for you and your team. But then you must turn the negative into a positive by analyzing the loss and improving on what you did wrong. Use loss as a way to grow and improve. We'll talk about this again in the next chapter because it's that important. "What does not destroy me makes me stronger." Smart words — and basketball was barely around yet!

YOU CAN NEVER LEARN HOW TO WIN UNTIL YOU LEARN HOW TO LOSE

Chapter Twelve:

IT'S HOW YOU REACT TO A LOSS

A fifty-four-year-old man was found to have a kidney mass, most likely a cancer that needed to come out. The patient, a father of three and a husband for twenty-seven years, was optimistic about his upcoming surgery. The procedure was considered routine, but because he had diabetes, my friend and fellow surgeon asked this man's primary care doctor to sign off. The doctor quickly consented, saying this patient took care of himself and had no reason to withhold or delay his treatment.

Anatomy appeared normal?	Yes.
Routine case?	Sure.
Concerned about outcome?	Always.

Only a few years before, urologic surgeons routinely used a twelve-inch incision through the flank to take out a kidney. These were big cases with large incisions, and often these patients stayed in the hospital for up to a week, with the recovery expected to be several months. My associate was fully trained in endourology. This meant that he could perform major urologic procedures through special tubes and small incisions, and as a result, the time it took patients to get back to routine activity was much shorter. This amazing and significant advancement required these surgeons to be deliberate, enduring, and meticulous in their technique — qualities my colleague had mastered.

The case went smoothly, in good time and without any untoward concern. There was no excessive bleeding, no unexpected findings, and the patient tolerated the procedure well. Two hours after the case was completed, the patient was back in his room, fully awake and talking normally with his family. My associate went back to his office for the day and then returned to the hospital to perform a quick check on his patient to see if anything else was needed. He found everything in order and the nurses reassured him saying they'd call if any issues came up. It had been a routine case, and everyone was happy.

A call did come from the nurses later that night, and it was not the usual request for more pain medication or a sleeping pill. The call came because the patient had just coded - meaning he had lost his pulse, was no longer breathing, and had no detectable blood pressure. The medical team had attempted a full resuscitation, but they were not successful, and the patient went on to die fairly quickly. My friend had the phone glued to his ear as he listened to the account, barely believing what he was being told. He then rushed over to the hospital, arriving in time to see his patient's lifeless body still in the same hospital bed where they had a last, comfortable conversation only a few hours before. It was almost surreal — the patient and his family had been so relieved only several hours earlier.

Doctors are human. We feel the pain and spend many sleepless nights second-guessing our decisions and questioning our surgical skills. That is, if you're a good doctor and care about getting better. This loss was profound for the patient's family, and that cannot be underemphasized. I will also tell you that it was incredibly painful for my colleague. He beat himself up continuously, wondering what he could have done differently and how he could have anticipated this horrible outcome. Taking full responsibility, he realized he would spend many nights pacing the floors of his home while his family slept. But because he was an experienced surgeon, he also knew time would eventually heal this open wound — certainly quicker for him than for the grieving family. In addition, he realized that it was essential that he deal with the loss as quickly as possible to help his other patients. He had to learn from this experience, to grow as a surgeon and as a person, and move on. That's just what was necessary, but that's also a situation when the pain gets worse before getting better.

The family had agreed to an autopsy, and my colleague requested to be present in the room when this happened. Having known the patient well before and witnessing his body being dissected after his death made this even more painful. In the days before the autopsy, my associate spent hours carefully reviewing the records from the case. He looked at the entire preoperative assessment for clues that, even in retrospect, would have helped predict the outcome. He studied the notes from the OR and the hours after, and then taking it one step further, he asked me to give my opinion and evaluate all the notes objectively, insisting that I be brutally honest if the slightest discrepancy was found. During that time, he went on to interview the primary care physician, the anesthesiologist, and the nursing staff who took care of the patient as well.

All postoperative deaths must be reviewed by a quality committee at the hospital, and when this case was studied, no errors were found. When I reviewed the records, I couldn't find anything that looked remotely out of line. My associate, being the toughest critic of all, found nothing that he would have done differently, even in retrospect.

Surgeons who don't understand that some things just can't be controlled or predicted will have a rough time as their career progresses. They need to learn early that even if you do everything right, the patient still might not do well. That's just a reflection on how complex the human body is. To be effective, physicians also need to understand that there are other forces we can't control; otherwise, a loss will paralyze our efforts on future cases. As painful as it was, my colleague faced his failure head-on. He critically studied each step, understanding well that if he had found an avoidable mistake, even in retrospect, he would use this to become a better doctor.

Loss Is Inevitable
How You React Will Define You

• • •

No one is perfect, and no one should expect to be. You won't always do what's right, and you will not always have a great game. Analyze and learn from each experience to be a better player, a better teammate, and a better person. Our freshman year, we won the first fifteen games before we suffered our first loss to an inferior team. I missed a shot at the end of the game that would have allowed us to win. My response to the loss was going home and locking myself in the bedroom to sulk, not speaking with anyone for several days. I thought this was how you learn from a loss, but I couldn't have been more wrong. My parents threatened to take me off the team, for which I was the starting point guard. They were right. At that point, I needed to understand how to lose correctly to eventually gain any level of future success. Fortunately, this did eventually happen. As was obvious and expected, my colleague was much further along with his understanding of loss and complications of surgery, and he responded properly. As a result of this distressing loss and terrible pain, he would grow to become a better surgeon and physician. Loss will always occur on the court and in your life, but it's how you respond to it that defines you.

LOSS IS INEVITABLE
HOW YOU REACT WILL DEFINE YOU

Chapter Thirteen:

HOW TO RECOGNIZE A GREAT COACH

"Coach, whenever I'm at a game now, all I hear is yelling from the bench. Why don't I ever remember that with you?"

"That's because I never yelled," Coach Blindow told me. "Never saw the reason. You guys made the decisions on the floor; I just had to get you prepared before that time during practice. If I did my job, I barely had to do anything come game time."

"But how did we reach that point?" I asked. "How were we able to run the game ourselves?"

"Bruce, it was all about practice and all those years learning the fundamentals. You all knew what to do. I don't think I ever did anything during a game that made you win or caused you to lose. It was always about the players."

This recent conversation with Coach Blindow amazed me in how well-thought-out his coaching style was — and how great a coach he had been for that reason. He had emphasized the need to learn the fundamentals from an early age, and with our discussion he reminded me of his favorite saying:

CAN'T SHOOT ... CAN'T PLAY!

Meaning that no matter your position on the court, you had to be able to contribute and shoot the ball. That was our job. We all had learned the proper technique, and it was each player's responsibility to perfect the shot. When called on during a game, you had to be able to score to secure any meaningful minutes. No one could afford to be a liability. That was understood.

Commitment, Practice, Focus, Discipline

Being able to shoot the ball was considered basic, and it was your responsibility to learn to shoot and to handle the ball. That was easy since we'd been taught that properly by Coach Blindow many years before. All we needed was a driveway or a basement. It was easy to dribble the ball walking around town, going to and from school, or going anywhere else. The playground was well used and there were hoops attached to most garages. We all loved to shoot and practiced whenever we could. It was important to feel completely connected to the ball.

•

In addition to shooting and ball handling, we also had learned to play tough defense, and always man-to-man. Defense takes communication. Defense takes effort and trust — trust in your-self and trust in your teammates. Most impor-tantly, defense takes pride. You have to want to stop your man from scoring, from playing better than you and beating your team. We were taught that there's never a reason to play poor defense. Your shot may not always fall and your timing may be off, but you still can make a difference on the other end of the floor. Learn this well - you should never have a bad night on defense.

These are just some of the fundamentals Coach Blindow taught us. There are other reasons to seek out and learn from a great coach, and these are summarized as follows:

A Great Coach Invests in You, Influences You, and Improves Your Game — and Your Life

• • •

I was fortunate in that Coach Blindow was a great coach. I did not recognize it at the time, but it's clear that my life would have followed a different path if not for his influence. That statement alone defines a great coach. With travel basketball and an abundance of opportunity for outside instruction, players today have access to any number of coaches who, if picked correctly, can change your life. That's why it's important to choose your coach wisely and keep them as a part of your life. Also, shy away from those who are not helpful, if at all possible.

So, how do you recognize a great coach? Let's further pool together some solid definitions.

- A great coach is a great teacher

- A great coach is a role model

- A great coach teaches a joy for the game

- A great coach teaches fundamentals

- A great coach teaches trust in team

- A great coach teaches earned confidence

- A great coach is an advocate for his players

To quote UCLA coach John Wooden about the highest compliment a coach can ever receive:

"One of the finest things a player could say about me after he left the team was that I cared every bit as much about him as an individual as I cared about him as an athlete."

That's how to recognize a great coach!

A GREAT COACH INVESTS IN YOU, INFLUENCES YOU, AND IMPROVES YOUR GAME — AND YOUR LIFE

Chapter Fourteen:

WRITE YOUR OWN STORY

The goal of this book is to teach you how commitment and passion are essential to reach any level of success. We also looked at the hours required for you to become skilled, highlighting the discipline that's required. Yet with this extensive commitment, does it mean if you never play in college or become a pro ballplayer, it was all just a waste of time and effort? Absolutely not! Let's see how the path itself, if pursued with true conviction, can change everything.

Remember that first you have to begin your journey without fear of the end result. Work hard and commit without reservation.

NEVER FEAR FAILURE

Most of us are convinced that we begin our path toward most goals at a disadvantage compared to our peers, and this makes us feel unsettled. The reality is that very few of us are completely confident when tackling a goal for the first time, unless of course this confidence is unearned and unrealistic, which we know is not a good trait. Walking onto a court early in my basketball career, I shuddered to witness the confidence of the other players, wondering if I'd ever reach that same level. I was also intimidated entering the classroom at Northwestern University for the first time and meeting the already accomplished premed students I'd be competing against. This reaction is normal. You just can't let it affect your playing ability or derail your progress. We all start from a different point, and chances are overwhelming that you're fine from where you are beginning. Don't look at others; stay focused, stay determined, and make smart decisions based on your own goals.

WE ALL START SOMEWHERE
WE ALL HAVE CHOICES TO MAKE

It's great to dream. It's great to dream big and spend a lot of time dreaming. Think about who you are and what you want to do with your life — meaning where you want to be the next year, in the next five years, and maybe even in the next ten. But after you're done dreaming (and that should happen fairly quickly), come up with a plan. This plan should be based on realistic expectations. Then be methodical and set your course, keeping in mind that these goals now have deadlines, objectives you will need to complete. This works for basketball and this works for life.

DREAMS ARE IMPORTANT, BUT GOALS HAVE DEADLINES

With your goals in place and your trek now in full swing, how do you take it to the next level? Let's remember the order:

- First, have a dream

- Next, make the commitment

- Third, have good teachers

- Fourth, be a good student

- And last, practice, practice, practice

Now is the time when the path becomes demanding, but it's also when your character is shaped. Now you'll discover who you are and get an idea of what you can accomplish. Finally, and probably most importantly at this time, is that you need to focus.

FOCUS

Focus - what exactly does this mean? Why is learning to focus essential, and why do I emphasize this concept? To focus means to direct your efforts and to concentrate, meaning to converge and to not back down. The ability to focus takes discipline, and very few people have that skill or care enough to develop it. The answer is that discipline is the key. Learn to focus, learn to be disciplined, and you'll be way ahead with all your goals. Never allow a poor outing or bad situation devastate you. Stay on track:

TAKE IT TO THE NEXT LEVEL
TURN A NEGATIVE INTO A POSITIVE

Dreams, goals, practice, focus, discipline. With all of this, you are striving to be perfect. Yet we all know being perfect will never happen. Ironically, it doesn't matter. Being perfect has nothing to do with the outcome of the game or even with your individual performance. Being perfect is knowing that you worked to your highest level to achieve the goal that was established. There will be setbacks and poor decisions along the way, but that's fine. That's expected. Being perfect means being able to look your teammates and coaches in the eyes and knowing without hesitation that you did all you could to achieve the goal. And most important, it means looking at yourself in the mirror and seeing the same. Becoming perfect is a process, and it doesn't only apply to the game you just played. It involves the weeks and months and years of preparation to reach that point. It takes time. It takes 10,000 hours. That's how you become perfect. That's how, after all that work you've invested, you begin to hold a deep confidence that no one can take away.

BECOMING PERFECT TAKES 10,000 HOURS

As a high school athlete, as I've emphasized, when I walked into almost every gym knowing my commitment and the hours I'd logged, I never doubted my ability. I knew that I could handle myself on the court. Today, walking into the operating room, I have the same feeling. My adrenaline may be pumping (just as it had before a tough game), but knowing the commitment and time that I have already put in allows the confidence to be there as well. I don't doubt my ability, and this reflects the earned confidence we've spoken about: the hours and hours of working and studying that allows you to understand without hesitation that you've gained the skill to handle most situations. And on that rare occasion that the challenge is beyond your scope, you've learned how to tuck your ego aside and call in the better player for backup. Again, how do you reach this level? It takes time, it takes commitment, and it takes an honest understanding that you did everything you could to get there.

CONFIDENCE MUST BE EARNED

There are many ballplayers with stellar individual stats, but their teams will never win. They take a ton of shots and usually are the high scorer, but know nothing about team play. They also get angry at their teammates, thinking they're not good enough. These players believe that no one else can play the game at their level, yet in reality, the problem is on them. They lack the ability to elevate their teammates' game, the unique skill to make other players better. Like everything else, growth starts in practice, where you learn to play together, learn to trust each other, and work toward each player's strengths. It's the coach's responsibility to establish this culture within the team, but even one or two selfish players can sabotage this effort. Basketball and life are hard enough, and we all need help. We need to cover for one another, work toward the same goal, and have pride in that concept.

TEAM FIRST ALWAYS

Few teams go undefeated. I'm convinced that it benefits a team to lose just before a major tournament. It allows that squad to see their weaknesses and adjust. It helps them realize that winning takes effort and is not always inevitable. Losing teaches so much more than winning. It highlights your character and demonstrates how to improve — that is, if you're willing to look for the answers and work on those weaknesses. In the best of circumstances and after every game, your team should ask the question, "How can we get better?" You will need to look at what you didn't do well, which is painful and takes discipline. But that's how you learn and grow.

A friend of mine serves as a navy fighter pilot. He eloquently explained that after each one-hour practice mission, he and his team will debrief for at least two hours to see how they could have worked the flight better.

- Were there any safety issues?

- Did the equipment function well?

- How could we have improved the mission?

In this scenario, more time is spent analyzing than actually doing. He explained that's how they learn and get better with every mission.

When I was a surgical resident, we routinely had a conference in surgery called M&M. That stands for surgical Morbidity and Mortality. This was a conference where any unexpected result or poor outcome was presented and examined in an honest and often brutal way.

- "Why did the surgery take so long?"

- "Didn't you know the patient had a bleeding disorder?"

- "What could you have done in retrospect that may have changed the outcome?"

- "What poor decision led to the patient's death?"

- "What would you do differently the next time?"

These were incredible learning experiences, even though our egos were often beaten up badly. Unfortunately, most hospitals stopped these valuable conferences; I'm told because the information could be shared with medical malpractice attorneys and result in huge lawsuits that may or may not have merit. Regardless, the honesty and learning from this open forum was stopped, which has not benefitted patient care.

You'll Never Learn How to Win until You Learn How to Lose

Loss Is Inevitable How You React Will Define You

There's a lot to learn when pursuing a passion, and of course with any challenge, there will be setbacks along the way. Staying focused and learning from the best teacher is important, and this is where coaches and role models are crucial. It's nice to have someone working with you who prioritizes your success. They should want you to succeed in life, even more than on the court, understanding that the two are not mutually exclusive. You will work with many people as you pursue your basketball career, and it's important to identify a great teacher and latch on. Learn all you can from this mentor. Use the criteria and definitions we went over, keeping in mind:

A GREAT COACH INVESTS IN YOU, INFLUENCES YOU, AND IMPROVES YOUR GAME — AND YOUR LIFE

Finally, you need to "write your own story," but what exactly does this mean, and why is this important? To "write your own story" means to chart your own course and influence your own life. Make your life happen by doing and not just allowing life to happen to you. Influence your existence and your path. Dream your dreams, set your goals, chart your course. Learn to be confident by putting in the time; take control, understand how to learn from setbacks, and choose your teachers well. Surround yourself with good people and good role models. Stay away from bad influences; they will bring you down. In other words:

WRITE YOUR OWN STORY

• • •

You've made the decision to play basketball. That's great; now embrace it. Put in the time, maintain the focus, and work to become the best you are capable of becoming. That dream and push may ultimately land you a D1 scholarship with a professional contract afterward. Amazing. Or you may find yourself sitting on the end of the bench for a mediocre jayvee team. That's great, too. The point is that it doesn't matter. As you push, and as you grow as a player, you are affecting your path and learning life skills that you will carry forever. Work hard, make adjustments, and focus to take control, and you will become the author of your own story. It will change you, I promise. For now, and most importantly, concentrate on learning the game. The rest will follow.

Good luck! I know that you will be very successful.

—BR

Acknowledgments

First, I would like to strongly acknowledge Coach Bill Blindow for his tremendous influence and also thank him for his assistance in this book. With his hammering home the fundamentals and his keen understanding of the game, we all thought that we were learning to be good basketball players. But it was so much more. Coach Blindow taught a generation of young ballplayers in Metuchen, New Jersey, and his presence lives on within this generation, the next, and those after that as well. He set the bar very high for future coaches.

Thanks to Coach Ari Zito for his brilliant basketball mind and possibly even greater skills as a teacher. To Coach Eric Acra for generously including me as a part of his team and demonstrating what it takes to be an incredible coach while holding unwavering principles. Also thanks to Coach Chris Williams, a person that can not only break down a game to make everyone play better but who does so after a long day saving the world. Not bad.

Thanks to Coach Tony Collins, who gave me my first opportunity in my second career and knows how to push old-school values. Also to Coach Caleb Henderson, who has a world of potential and only great things in store for his future.

To the devoted and skilled sportswriter John Haley. I thank you for taking the time to help me with this project and our many conversations on how basketball can and did change a lot of lives. You were always a great teammate. Thanks to Ed Iannarella for your assistance and for being an exceptional role model and always being strong, focused and supportive. Thank you to North-western Coach Pat Fitzgerald, for being so generous with his time and imparting wisdom and principals that are important for any team and for any organization. Go 'Cats!

Thank you to Jennifer Rockwell on her review of the manuscript and allowing me to bounce ideas off on a weekly basis and Liz Wakefield for her profound insights on the project. Also thanks to Cameron Rosenberger for his assistance and opinion in the very early stages and having an amazing love for the game. Just as important, an acknowledgment and thanks to my editors, Jennifer Schuster and Christina Roth. Without your expertise, this book could never happen.

Last, and in no way least, a great thank you to my wife, Lisa, for her support, love of books and her amazing ability to edit. You made this project something to be proud of.

CPSIA information can be obtained
at www.ICGtesting.com
Printed in the USA
LVHW111703011119
635934LV00005B/313/P